Dr. Delores T. Henderson

XULON PRESS

Xulon Press
2301 Lucien Way #415
Maitland, FL 32751
407.339.4217
www.xulonpress.com

Author's Note: As it relates to articles that were utilized as references, please note that those writers may or may not agree with the author's views or philosophy. The views expressed in this book may not be the views of the writers of the articles. They are the views and personal experiences of the author.

Printed in the United States of America.

ISBN-13: 9781545648797

BIOGRAPHY OF

Dr. Delores T. Henderson

Ambassador Dr. Delores T. Henderson was born, raised, and educated in Washington, DC. She is the mother of Ms. Wakita Mone' Henderson, who she cites since her daughter's birth, "my inspiration," and very proud grandmother of Ms. Gabrielle Kaylen Singleton.

Ambassador Dr. Henderson is the Founder & CEO of the Survivors' Global Ministry (SGM), a non-profit charitable organization that has programs such as: Help for the Homeless, Intervention on behalf of Suicidal Victims, Help for Abused Women and Children, and several Outreach Programs. She is also the Founder & CEO of Virtue Consulting Company and Dr. DTH Ministries, Inc. She is a Radio Personality hosting her show "Straight to the Point", a broadcast that is aimed at dealing with real issues and offering real solutions that face our society domestically and internationally. She is the Television Personality & Executive Producer of TV Show, "The Right Now Word" which airs on the Eternal Life Network. She is an Author that has authored several books, which includes, Misguided Affections, When A Prophet Cries Something Happens, and I Give You Keys. She is the originator of the "Moving Mountains" Conference Line. She Founded the SGM Bible College and School of the Prophets. She built from the ground and served as the Co-Founder & Vice President of The Rhema School of the Prophets (RSOP) Largo, MD. She served as a Business Consultant and Advisor to the International Alliance Ministry of Servants (IAMS).

Ambassador Dr. Henderson holds a Doctor of Divinity Degree with the honors of Kingdom Ambassadorship-At Large & Chaplain. She has earned credits towards a Doctor of Education in Organizational Leadership Degree. She currently holds a Master of Theological Studies (MTS), a Master of Business Administration (MBA), and a Bachelor of Science (BSBA) in Business Administration degrees. She attended and graduated from the Rhema Bible College, under the leadership of Apostle, Dr. Richard L. Archer, Largo, MD. She has earned other ministerial education, training and credits from the Crown of Christ Bible Institute, under the leadership of Pastor Patricia Tyous. She also had ministry training with the International

Alliance Ministry of Servants (IAMS) "Missions" field, under the leadership of Dr. Deborah Nelson. She is a member and partner of the International Congress of Churches & Ministers, also known as ICCM, located in Chattanooga, TN.

Although she had been preaching, teaching, and spreading the Gospel since 2004, Ambassador Dr. Henderson did not receive her License to Minister until August 2006, with the International Alliance Ministry of Servants, under the Leadership of Dr. Deborah Nelson and Bishopric of George Bloomer, Bishop of C.L.U.R.T. (Come Let Us Reason Together). She was featured on the magazine, "Focus On Women". She was also featured on the cover and in the September 2015 issue of "Majesty Now" magazine. Ambassador Henderson had also been featured on the "Preach The Word Worldwide Network" as well had been nominated & received the "Shining Star" Award. She is also known as an "expert" and has been awarded for her excellent entrepreneurship skills.

A Prophet in her mother's womb, Ambassador Dr. Henderson was Ordained as a Prophet in the Lord's Church on July 24, 2010. She has served on several out-reach ministries under the leadership of Dr. Deborah Nelson. She has traveled to International countries such as Belgium, Europe in 2004, Kenya, East Africa (2005 & 2007 & 2014, 2017), preaching and teaching the Word of God to underprivileged men, women, and children in Mombasa and the village of Taita Hills, Kenya, East Africa, and London, United Kingdom in 2015, Birmingham, United Kingdom in 2018. She continues her work in the land of Africa on a continual basis partnering with her several leaders to ensure the gospel is spread all over the world.

- Misguided Affections
- I Give You Keys
- When A Prophet Cries: Something Happens

<u>Purchase ALL Three At:</u>

- Xulonpress.com
- Amazon.com
- Barnesandnobles.com
- Appleibooks.com
- Deloresh30.wixsite.com/drdthministries
- drdthministries@gmail.com or 240-676-32

DEDICATION

This book is dedicated to every Entrepreneur, Mentor, Teacher, Spiritual Leader, Counselor and Coach. You all are needed in the lives of people who want to effect change. Changing the world is not easy, but with guidance and wise counsel, lined up with determination, consistency and hard-work, "Nothing Is Impossible for Them That BELIEVE.

This book is dedicated to every mother, father, son, daughter, sister, brother, niece, nephew, cousin, aunt, uncle, grandparent, god-parent, god-child, friend and associate. I encourage you to KEEP Shining to the point that no one would be able to say they do not see you. Shine through the clouds and shine through the rain. Whatever you do and whatever it takes, just SHINE.

This book is also dedicated to every person who will invest and read this winner (book). You are important, and YOU Are Not A Mistake. You were Purposed to do great and marvelous works right here in the Earth. You have "Super Powers"; and those Powers, if discovered and utilized properly will bring you to a place called

Destination, in which you will find yourself living and being "Your Best Self Yet".

Lastly, on paper, but not last in my heart, this book is dedicated to my daughter, Wakita M. Henderson and granddaughter, Gabrielle K. Singleton. I want to also dedicate this book to my god-daughters, Donika Burrows, Kenyatta Malloy, and JoeNya Jones. I want to encourage my girls, and to let them know, the Sky is not even the limit for them. And that Nothing is hard for anyone that believes! Keep going ladies, I am in your corner!

TABLE OF CONTENTS

INTRODUCTION

Are you at a place in your life where you are wondering what your purpose is? Are you asking yourself at this very moment, what should I be doing? Who should I be connecting with? Why is life so hard? When will it get easier? Why did this happen? And why did this person leave and or why didn't this person go?

Life can be a big giant puzzle if you do not know what your purpose is. You will find yourself walking in circles, spinning on the same merry-go-round, running on the same road, but staying in the same spot if you are not sure of and or have knowledge of your purpose. Knowing your purpose in life is crucial for great success. Once you know your purpose you can begin to move in the right direction, walk on the right road, and connect with the right people.

If you are living, breathing, and reading this book I want you to know that you have a purpose. The definition of purpose according to the Oxford Living Dictionary, "the reason for which something is done or created or for which something exists" (https://en.oxforddictionaries.com). You were not born just to exist, but you were born to make a difference. You were born to effect change. You were born to break glass ceilings. You were born to break records. And most importantly, you were born to make a difference in someone else's life.

We are great when we help others become great. Difference makers, history makers, and legends were not given those titles just because they became great all by themselves. They had someone to help them, whether that was in the form of a coach, mentor, teacher, parent, counselor, or a friend, they had people to help them reach different levels which led them to the place of greatness. You noticed I said levels. It is important to know that success does not happen overnight, nor does greatness. There is a process in which we recognize, identify, and grow. In the process of recognize, one must first recognize and know their worth. In the process of identify, one must be able to identify who they are first. What drives you? What motivates you? In the process of growth, one must know that growth is vital in the development of their goals, dream, or promise. Therefore, never stop learning. Keep moving towards and working on the goal no matter the burden or the pressure to quit or to give up.

Connecting with the right people can help you go far in life and may even help you reach your goals at a more-faster rate. Identifying and being able to discern people who were sent into your life to be a blessing is important. Weeding out those who do not have your best interest from those who do will allow you to build and reach your goals surrounded by people who love, care and genuinely want to see you succeed. It is vital to have a strong network of people who you can learn from, get counsel and or direction when you yourself need guidance.

There was as saying that Rome was not built overnight. Therefore, if you are looking for microwave success, you will be sadly disappointed. Yes, I believe in miracles, but even the creator tells us that to have great success we must put in the work. Many successful people, those that are self-made multi-millionaires will tell you of the countless nights they did not sleep because they were working on their dream. They will tell you and be happy to share with you the many sacrifices that they had to make to see their dream come into fruition. Some were homeless. Some lost families. Some had to sleep in cars. All because they believed in their dream. And in reading all the success stories, none of it happened over night. There were many tears shed, many battles fought, and many lonely days and nights. And many times, they even questioned should they continue. However, one thing for sure, they all had one thing that kept them going, and that was their dream.

At the end of the day, how fast you get there relies on you. You are the author of the dream. You are the visionary. You must believe in yourself and your dream when no one else believes in the dream, you do. You must have the drive that if no one else sees it, you see it. If no one else believes you, you believe. If no one else will go, you will go. If everyone leaves, you will stay.

It all balls down in knowing you. Who are you? You must be able to convince yourself that even the stars are not unreachable. Will you allow those around you to discourage you from reaching the stars? Will you allow even your own doubts to stop you from reaching the stars? Many times, we can be our own greatest enemy. We look for enemies around us, but if truth be told, only you can stop your dream from coming to pass.

Many things such as self-doubt, lack of knowledge, insecurities, self-hatred, and the four Ds stop progress and growth. The four Ds comprise of Doubt, Dismay, Discouragement and Distraction. When you allow the four Ds to rise and or enter in, dreams are stalled. Doubt is a killer all by itself. Doubt is when someone allows his or her own mind to talk them out of their blessing, purpose and or promise. Yes, I said, their own minds. When working towards a goal or dream, and when met with difficulty, many starts doubting their abilities. Dismay starts to work in, and before you know it a state of distress overcomes the person. After dismay, discouragement starts talking to the person, and before you know it, the dream is put on hold or the goal is not met. Then your friend name distraction comes along looking grand. Distractions looks glimmer and glowing, and before you know it, you are wanting what someone else has and you forget all about the vision, dream, and purpose and promise that was given to you. You stop working on your goals and start working on and or with other people's goals. And years and years pass, and your dream is in the same place at the same point in where you left it. All because you did not deal with the four Ds that were inside of you. The enemy in you.

Having a lack of knowledge is also detrimental to your success and is a big enemy within. Not knowing how to conduct something and or the reason behind it, and trying to go out and do it, can harm you and other people. It is important to learn as much as you can about you first, your passion, your trade, your talent and your gift before you offer it to anyone else.

Insecurities can stop good and productive relationships. Remember, connecting with people who have the resources to take you to the next level is very important. However, if you are racked with insecurities, you will miss the benefit and advantage of having built strong relationships to carry you in your season of "is it still mines"?

What do I mean about your season of “is it still mines”? No matter how strong your faith is, there is always going to be a season in your life where you are going to ask, “is it still mines”? And you are going to need strong formidable people around you who are proven and who have made it to the level of success in which they can encourage, motivate and push you forward. However, if you are insecure, you will run those people away from you.

Self-hatred is another enemy within. It can also be known as low self-esteem. What you think of yourself matters how far you will go in life. No one wants to be around someone who is always talking down about themselves. Remember, you must be your most avid supporter. You must be your most ardent cheerleader. If you do not believe in yourself or your abilities, you will find yourself connecting with folks who only feed your ego and not your intellect.

There was a saying that stated, “we attract who we are”. Therefore, to attract greatness, you should think of yourself as great. If you want to attract success, you should think of yourself as successful. I heard of another saying, “you are what you think”. If you think you will never make it, you won’t make it. If you think you will never succeed, you won’t succeed. If you think you do not have what it takes to win, you won’t win. The goal is to change your thinking. Think on positive things. Thinks on pure things. Read books that challenge you to think right. Connect with people that motivate you to live right.

The goal is to win, but first win within. Before you can win without, you got to win within. Know who you are. Know your purpose. Know the reason behind the purpose. Know the resources you to need to help you meet that purpose. Once you know what you know and how to utilize that know, you will find yourself being Your Best Self Yet!

CHAPTER I

The Road to Discovering You

The road that leads you to the place of discovery can feel like you are walking outer space. Some days you may feel as if you are not moving. And some days you may feel you have tried everything possible, but still no change. Change can be troubling for some, and many people fight against it. However, it is change that allows a person to evolve into greatness. When I think about change and how important it is for everyone, I think about a new born baby. Yes, how that baby grows into a beautiful toddler. And the one thing that excites me is the courage, determination, and will the toddler have to walk. No matter how many times the toddler falls, with determination, that toddler gets back up and tries repeatedly until the toddler masters the craft of walking. That toddler has just done something major, and that is discovered how to walk. It is important to know the same way that toddler refused to lose, you must have that same mindset and simply walk to your road of discovery.

Many people try to fix themselves up before stepping out on faith, but it will not be faith if you try to put things in order or even wait until things are in perfect order before you step out to accomplish your dream. Many times, the journey is long because you refuse to give up apart of you that does not want to adjust. Some situations cause for adjustments. It goes back to always learning, being open, and able to adapt.

Discovering you and who you really are and not what others want you to be can take a while if you refuse to face reality. And that reality can be hurtful when looking back at your life, and you come to the realization that your living has been to please people, and not yourself; to go above and beyond for people and forget about your needs; to try and make everyone else happy, even at the expense of your unhappiness, and you neglect your responsibilities, to help others and their responsibilities. All the while your goals and dreams are just waiting for you to remember them. They are yelling in your mind both day and night, remember me.

The power of agreement on your road to discovering you is very important. First and foremost, you must come to a place of inner agreement. Are you fighting with yourself? Are you wrestling with your own thoughts and feelings about the road and or are you on the right road? These are all familiar questions that each person must come to terms with, especially if they believe they have been on the same road for a long time. Sometimes the will, intellect and body conflict with each other. They are totally not in agreement, but the goal is to make them all come to a place of agreement.

The body is always in a fight with the will and the intellect. The body rarely wants to walk on any road. The body rarely wants to do anything that would take it out of its comfort zone. However, for the walk to even occur, the will have to take dominance and command the body to line up.

The intellect can be very tricky because it fights the will and the body with book knowledge. It tries to throw the will and body off by reminding the will what history states, what books states, what doctors states, and what science states. However, to reach your goals, you are going to have forego all of what anything states and get on that road and walk towards discovering you.

The will wants what it wants. The will is the place that allows you to keep going on no matter what it looks like, tastes like or feels like. The will keeps you strong, built in faith, and going on. It is the will that in the face of the adversity ensures success. It is the will that speaks to the intellect and the body and command both to come into alignment and agreement with destiny. It is your will that will ensure total discovery and victory. It is your will that will keep you on the road when your feet grow weary. It is your will that will keep you on the road when your shoes wear out. It is your will that will keep you on the road when you hit a pot hole. It is your will that will keep you on the road when you find yourself walking all alone. And it will be your will that will keep you on the road when you feel uneasy, discouraged, and like you have walked your last mile.

The uneasiness you feel while on the road to discovering you is the feeling of wanting to please others, and the voice that has lied to you, and have called you a failure. To reach the destination, you are going to have to blot out the voices. The only voices you should be allowing in your memory are the voices that are in tune with your voice, which is the voice of unity. United voices, meaning your inner voice and the outer voices are all speaking the same tune. And what I mean by this is, you all are on one accord, positive, believe in the vision, and agree.

There is power in unity, but only failure in discord and division. If you believe you are on the right road moving towards self-discovery, reaching your goals and fulfillment of dreams, but those (outer voices) you have walking with you are in total disagreement, get rid of them. Those outer voices are the reason why you are still in the same place. Just like there is positive power in unity, there is negative power in disagreement and discord. You must decide which power you are going to allow drive you towards your goals because only positive power can lead you to great success.

You and you alone can stop yourself from becoming all you should ever become in life. I wrote about voices, but there is only one voice that is the strongest out of them all and that is the voice of self-destruction. The loudest voice you will ever have to defeat is the one known as the voice of self-destruction. This voice badgers you and is the one in your head that tells you to give up. The one that tells you to quit. The one that tells you the dream will never come to pass, or the vision is not strong. This voice comes to do one thing, and that is to destroy you. Did you notice I wrote self-destruction? Yes, no outside force is to blame for this action. While on the road to discovering you, you will find that certain actions can cause self-destruction. Actions such as deciding to not forgive yourself from past failures and or mistakes; deciding not to forgive others; rehearsing in your mind what others have done to you and refusing to let it go; bitterness; covetous; jealousy and trying to walk in shoes that are too big for you. These actions will stop you dead in your tracks and you will find yourself in a halt. You will find yourself not moving along at all, and most of all you will find yourself walking in circles.

You must let go of that inner voice in your head, as well as people, places and things that cause you to hold on to unforgiveness. It all balls down to making the decision to forgive. It is crucial that you forgive yourself for any bad decision or action you may have committed against yourself or someone else. Unforgiveness will have you walking in shame and will cause you to make bad decisions based on past mistakes and failures. Forgiveness is a part of the journey. When you learn to first forgive yourself, forgiving others will come as natural as running water.

Bitterness is rooted in you because of holding on to unforgiveness. Refusing to let go of the offense or the situation that has caused you to harbor these feelings will cause self-destruction. Once you forgive yourself, quickly forgive others, and let it go. Forgiving others makes you free. It allows you to move on with your life without harboring ill-will and hatred in your heart. Harboring these things will cause you to build faulty relationships. If you do not forgive others, you will find your relationships of all kinds built on suspicion, lack of trust, and unproductive.

When you covet another person's gift, fame, fortune, or position, you will find yourself on the road to self-destruction. When you are walking on your road and looking at someone else on their road, and it looks like that person is just smooth sailing and you are barely able to stand up, this can make you want to jump on their road. When you know who you are there is no room or time to want what someone else has. Remember, the grass always looks greener on the others side. You have no idea what that person had to do to keep that grass green. When you are on your road it always looks like someone else's road is easier. The best thing for you to do is to keep your eyes on your goals and on your own road. Do not look to the left or the right, but look straight ahead, simply keep your eyes on the target.

While walking on your road to self-discovery, you must know that you are unique, one of a kind, and that your purpose was tailored made for you. If you are not careful, you will find yourself walking in shoes too big for you. Too many times, people try to walk in other people shoes. There is no room for you in another person's shoes nor is there room for that person to be in your shoes. When something is tailored made for you no other person will be able to fit it. That means even if you both are the same size, weight and height, only that person will be able to fit what was tailored-made for them, and only you will be able to fit what was tailored made for you.

The road to discovering you is not a trip it is a journey. Walking on this road and having to come to the realization of who you are from who you thought you were can be rewarding to some and detrimental to others. It can be rewarding if you meet the challenges head on and adjust when needed. However, it can be detrimental when you refuse to accept reality and refuse to make the necessary changes to succeed and ultimately win.

The road to discovering you is a lifelong road. No one has mastered it. What I mean by no one has mastered it, I mean every day of your life no matter how old you are, you will always be walking in self-discovery. It is a lifelong process and as you get older, you grow wiser, stronger, and better. We all have a road to walk on. No matter how easy someone else's path may look to you, always remember only the person walking their road knows what they had to endure to be able to keep on walking. Nobody ever said the road would be easy, but if you keep walking, you will surely reach your destination. Remember, there is an end. And reaching that end depends only on you. You hold the keys to your destiny. The keys were given to you before the foundations of the world. Use your keys to discover the greatness within. Use your keys to unlock the treasures that are just waiting to spill over and take you to your wealthy place. Your wealthy place may be a place of peace. Your wealthy place may be a place of healing and wholeness. Your wealthy place may be a place of unspeakable joy.

Whatever that place is to you, remember you have the keys, in short, use them.

Many of you have gifts and talents that are just waiting for you to discover and learn of them. Yes, I said learn of them. These gifts and talents are there for you to utilize. They will help you obtain your promise. For you to discover these gifts and talents, you must put your feet to the fire. Meaning, you must get up and work. My favorite book says, “Faith without works is dead”, (King James Version, Holy Bible). That’s right. You can have all the faith, but if you do not put your faith into action all you would have is hope of evidence not seen. Meaning, you just see, but you did not get up to act on what it is that you have seen.

In the road to discovery, it is plain and simple, to get what it is that you see, you must get up and put in the work until it comes to pass. Do not stop working to entertain doubt. Do not stop working to entertain self-pity. Do not stop working to entertain accusations or lies but continue the work to the Road to discovering you, and you will find that what you were looking for, you already got it, and that in fact, it was already there. You already have joy. You already have peace. You already have prosperity. You already have faith. You already wealth. You just got to use what is in your hands. Use what is in your treasure box.

Pointers in The Road To Discovering You:

1. Do not stop learning
2. Let your will dominate your intellect and your body
3. The road to discovering you is not a trip it is a journey
4. Walk in your own shoes
5. Pay attention to your own road
6. Your trials and what you must endure is tailored made for you
7. You must put in the work
8. Do not covet another's road
9. You have gifts, talents and a treasure inside of you
10. It's in your hands

CHAPTER II

FACE YOUR FEARS

Once you have come to the realization of discovering yourself. You must begin to face your fears. Sometimes it is not easy to discover certain things about yourself that you did not know existed. You may have thought you were healed or delivered from a certain thing or situation, but only to find out years later, when it was time for you to deal with a certain matter, that the situation still existed. And in fact, it had not healed at all. Coming to terms and to grips about a certain issue can be frightening if you are not ready to deal with it. You must deal and come to terms with any issue, situation, or circumstance that will hinder you from becoming Your Best Self Yet.

Facing your fears is what I recommend to anyone who is endeavoring to accomplish goals, meet deadlines, and become them best selves. One issue that many suffer with is the fear of failure. Many people believe that failing is the number one reason for not starting business ventures or taking steps towards goals and fulfilling their dreams.

Fear is the absence of faith. Fear and faith cannot live in the same dwelling. Fear capitalizes and decapitates you. Meaning it takes over your mind and causes the rest of your body to follow it. The result is unproductivity, lack, poverty, unmet goals and an unfulfilled life.

Most people are unproductive because of sudden fear. They may have started on the goal; however, experienced a bump in the road that brought on a sudden fear to complete the task. Unproductivity not only brings on poverty but also hinders relationships. No one wants to be around anyone who is unproductive. Unproductivity is contagious. If you find people disconnecting from you, one of the reasons can be unproductivity. Remember, you attract what and who you are. If you want to be productive you must conquer your fears.

Fear brings on lack. If you have fears of starting on your goals and moving towards your goals, you will find yourself the borrower and the not the lender. You will find yourself always needing. You will find yourself never having enough. All because you have allowed fear to stop you from accomplishing the much-needed goals to succeed.

Fear can cause you to not meet goals. If you do not meet your goals, then success is just a fairytale. Meaning, in your mind, a day dream, all talk but no action. Fear of the unknown have caused many people to miss out on blessings. You must be able to face your giants head on, and if need to, take them out.

Fear can cause you to live an unfulfilled life. The whole moral of life is to be fulfilled. If you allow fear to cause unfulfillment, you will find yourself a very unhappy and lonely person. You will find yourself on many occasions discouraged, frustrated, and unsatisfied because you have allowed fear to keep you from living Your Best Life as well as Being Your Best Self Yet.

Fear can cause you to become displeased and disgruntled in relationships. You may become angry or upset of assumed and perceived communication. Perception is a killer alone. Therefore, when you perceive a thing, it does not necessarily mean that what you perceive is true. It can be your fears stopping you from seeing the clear picture of a matter or situation. Most people perceive things based on past experiences and fear.

Fear causes you not to have the real conversation surrounding your preconceived notions. Whenever you perceive or form a decision based on fear, automatically know that your intel is faulty, and you can end up hurting yourself and all parties involved. Relationships crash based on faulty intel. Faulty intel is a result of fear driven assumptions and accusations.

The fear of rejection can stop productive relationships. The fear that someone will reject you based on past issues and or unresolved issues will stop you in your tracks and cause you not to move forward. Fear makes you hide from the truth. Fear makes you cover up and hide behind veils. Fear makes you wear masks. Fear makes you go your whole life being someone that you are not. In the end, walking in fear not only hurt other people, but hurts you the most.

Whenever you hide who you really are to conform to the likes of a person or a group of people, you need to know that those are not the people that are assigned to your life. The people that are assigned to your life will love, care and appreciate the True you. The people that are assigned to your life will help you discover the Best in you.

When you are connected to the right people, you should be able to walk in freedom and not fear. Whenever you disguise yourself and pretend to be something or someone that you are not you are setting yourself up for failure. Matter of fact, you have already failed because you are walking and living a life of fairytale. Every relationship that was built on this false rendition of you will crash once the real you show up. Yes, the real you will show up one day, and when it does, the faulty relationships that were built will come crashing down.

The only way you can become Your Best Self Yet, is being true to you. You know yourself better than anyone else. You know if you are living a life of falsity. You know if you are living in truth or not. You know if you are walking in fear or fakeness. It is best for you to come clean and be free to be you, or simply adopt the saying "free to be me".

Yes, it is important to be free. It is important for your health, your mental state and for your success to walk in freedom and not in fear. Pretending to be something or someone you are not is a set up for disaster. It is best to put your foot forward and live a life without shame and regret. To live a life without shame and regret you must kick fear out of the door. You must bolt the door and command fear to never to return.

Fear will cloudy your mind and paralyze your dreams. Your thoughts will become clouded. Whenever you try to think of ideas and strategies, you will find yourself in a blank stare. Your mind becomes heavy and doubt will eat up your membranes. Paralysis will sit in and you will find yourself not being able to move readily from one place to another. You will find yourself stuck and not able to move freely without the assistance of others, all because you have allowed fear to control your mind and movements.

Face your fears head on. Cancel its appearance. Fire its employment and vacate its residence. When you face your fears head on, you take back your strength. You push past your emotions. You simply Win.

Confronting your giants is the last step of conquering fear. Many times, people try to hide from the battles they are faced with because of fear. When you confront your giants, and not hide, fear dissipates. Fear must scatter. Confronting your giants drives away fear. When you finally face that situation, circumstance, or person and or people You will start becoming Your Best Self Yet. Walking in courage and faith produces dispels and dissolves fear.

Confrontation is not a bad word. Many people hide from the word confrontations because of fear. Fear that the other person will see you confronting them as a negative connotation. Fear that something bigger will appear if you confront the person. However, confrontation is always good if it is done in a respectful manner. Yes, sometimes the other person may react in a negative way, but to get free, you are going to have to confront some things. Not confronting makes you bound. Not confronting makes you harbor unforgiveness. Not confronting and dealing with the issue head on, makes you walk in the fear of assumption.

What is the fear of assumption? The fear of assumption is making decisions guessing what and or how you feel the other person meant by what they did and or said, when you could had just simply asked them to clarify their statement. Too many people are walking around in the fear of assumption. And because of it, many business relationships are suffering, personal relationships are suffering, marital relationships are suffering. In short, you have a whole myriad of people walking around in the spirit of offense, mainly because of the fear of assumption. And because of fear, no one is brave enough to confront the other person to find out the truth or the reasoning behind their statements.

All in all, fear is the biggest obstacle in becoming your Best Self Yet. Fear is the biggest obstacle in becoming your best at anything. That is why when fear rises, it is best to immediately speak to it and command it to die. It is important to speak life to courage and faith afterwards.

Speaking death to fear should never be considered scary or ghostly. Speaking death to anything that will cause you to stumble and fall should be a daily regimen. Just as you speak death, speaking life should immediately follow. As you speak death to your fears, assumptions, preconceived notions, and doubts; you should speak life to your faith, truth, dreams, goals and strategies.

When facing your fears, you must walk in a boldness that not only confuse others but will also cancel out any left-over residue. Residue can be dangerous. It seeps back up when you think that it had disappeared. Just like a cut that heals on the top, but the under the surface the wound is wide open. You must ensure the residue has totally disappeared so that when you are faced with another seemingly obstacle, you will not hesitate to squash it under your feet.

In short, fear is not your friend. Fear is your enemy. It comes to rob you out of destiny. It comes to dominate and to destroy. However, if you dismantle it before it becomes apparent, you will prosper in every area of your life. You will prosper in every area of your life because as stated earlier, fear is the number 1 thing that will rob you of your destiny. Anything that would try to rob you of your purpose and destiny, immediately needs to be dismantled and destroyed.

Pointers In Facing Your Fears:

1. Face your fears head on
2. Do not Pretend to be something you are not
3. Step out on faith
4. Never hide behind the veils of life
5. Conquer your giants
6. Walk in boldness
7. Immediately dismantle and destroy
8. Speak death to fear and life to your freedom and faith
9. Do not be led by the fear of assumption
10. Fear is the biggest obstacle in becoming Your Best Self Yet

CHAPTER III

It All Starts with a Dream

I am sure by now I have gotten you thinking about your dreams and goals. You are probably feeling like you can kick down any door, fly high enough to touch the sky, and probably sleep on the moon. I would say there is nothing wrong with thinking high. There is nothing wrong with wanting to win. There is nothing wrong with wanting to succeed. And there is nothing wrong with having high expectations. The only other thing I would like to add, and to let you know, it all starts with dream.

What is your dream? What are you aspiring to do? What causes you to want to jump out of the bed early in the morning and start working on it? What motivates and drives you to stay up late at night working on it? What makes you continue working on it no matter how many times you've failed? Does whatever you are aiming for bring you joy? Does it make you want to work on it until you see the manifestations of your labor? If you have answered yes to all these questions, then you have a valuable dream.

Successful people don't wake up successful. Amazon did not become the world's richest company by merely existing. Microsoft did not just invent itself. Oprah Winfrey did not become rich and famous upon being birthed. Serena Williams did not become one of the greatest tennis players of all times by just waking up. Tyler Perry did not just roll over and his plays became some of the best plays ever written. Many of the legends we celebrate did not become legends overnight. Self-made millionaires and billionaires did not just become rich overnight. Every successful person all have one thing in common, they all had a dream, because it all starts with a dream.

What is your dream? What are you aspiring to do? What is it that you cannot seem to get out of your mind. You wake up with it on your mind, you day dream about it all during the day; you have night visions all through the night. Maybe you are dreaming about starting your own business. Maybe you have dreams to change the world. Maybe your dream is to become an Author. Maybe your dream is to become a billionaire. Whatever the case, it all starts with a dream.

Everyone on the Earth has been given gifts and talents to help them accomplish their goals and reach their dreams. The key is to find out what those gifts and talents are then unlock them with the power of Faith. After the discovery of your gifts and talents, you must find out what is the venture that you are most passionate about. Once you find the venture that you are passionate about, put a plan in place to help you reach those goals toward the fulfillment of the dream. You must write down your plan. I recommend writing down short-term and long-term goals. Every short-term goal prepares you for your long-term goal. And finally, step out on faith and work your plan. Work you plan until fulfillment.

Reading books about other's successes can be helpful. Researching and speaking to a mentor and coach can be very helpful as well. But be very careful who you share your dream with. Everyone will not be as excited as you. And those who may be excited, may be trying to steal your ideas. Therefore, be selective in who you choose to reveal your ideas and or plans to.

Mentors can steer you in the right direction. However, ensure you get counsel from mentors who have mastered the field in which you are interested in. I recommend this because those who have mastered the field will be able to provide wisdom, knowledge, insight, and direction to you. This insight, wisdom, knowledge and direction can save you a lot of wasted time, money, headaches, and failures. Would you go to a Doctor asking about legal issues? Would you go to the Dentist for foot pains? I am sure the answer is No to both of those questions, Neither would I.

If you are trying to reach a specific goal, it is important to connect with those that have accomplished just as much as you have, if not more. This is important because those people will have no reason to compete with you. They will have no reason to sabotage or want to see you fail. However, I am sure in some cases you will still find those with more, who still envy; and when you find yourself in those situations, immediately disconnect. When you are building you cannot afford to have enemies in the camp. You want to keep those people far away.

When you are building and working towards your dream, you cannot afford to listen to negativity or people who are doubting your abilities to complete the tasks, assignment or goal. You are going to need all the encouragement you can get because times will get hard. Therefore, you need people in your corner that believe in you. You need people that believe in the vision, but most importantly you got to believe in the vision.

No one will or should ever believe in your vision more than you do. If so, you can be persuaded. And the goal is not to be persuaded or to conform to what someone else would have you to. You are the visionary. It is your dream. It is your vision, and it is solely up to you to make it happen.

Making it happen means doing whatever (legally) you must do to see that dream come to pass. There are great sacrifices in seeing dreams come into fruition. However, if you want it bad enough you will succeed. You will overcome any obstacle that comes your way.

You will see it through. You must see it through because if you want to win in the end, you are going to have to reach deep in the inside of yourself and grab encouragement, motivation, and strength because there are going to be times when you feel as though you have none left. But you will do it, and you will do it because it's your dream.

After the plan and consulting with mentors you must count the cost. Yes, is it worth the investment? Your answer should be Yes. It is your dream, and your dream is more than worth the investment. If you do not believe the dream is worth the investment how would you get others to believe your dream is worth the investment?

Counting the cost also means figuring out what type of funding you are going to need to get this dream off the ground. Counting the cost means finding out who are the people, what are the places and things, that are needed to help make this dream a success. All those things should be considered because what you do not want to happen is you start and cannot complete because of a lack of resources.

There are so many resources out here to help you with your dream. These resources are just waiting for you to reach out and grab them. Many times, people miss out on funding and important resources because of a lack of knowledge. People who suffer from having a lack of knowledge, is stopped from being successful. To succeed, you must utilize every resource possible.

There is no room for pride when you are in business or trying to reach a goal or fulfill a dream. You must put the pride aside, roll those sleeves up and ask for help where help is needed. You must have a mindset that everybody is a customer. Yes, everyone you meet no matter where is a potential customer, member, consumer, or tenant.

Every fulfilled anything requires needing assistance one way or another. You biggest resource is people. If you are in business for yourself, you must learn to communicate will all people. Mastering people can be hard if you are not dealing with or interacting with people daily. However, to stay in business and to succeed in business you must learn the art of dealing with people. You may not ever master people, but you must learn how to adjust your habits and personality to ensure respectful communication is exhibited. The goal is to always end up in a "win win" situation. Everyone should come out feeling they've won. If you can accomplish this, the battle has been won.

Mastering yourself is more important than mastering others. It is important that you learn how to master your emotions, master your opinions, and master your mouth. Mastering your emotions is important because people are going to say things that are going to crush your spirit, but you are going to have to learn how to swallow those feelings and keep it moving. Mastering your opinions is just as important. There are going to be times where people are going to say stupid, idiotic things, and you are going to want to blast them with your opinion on the matter, but you must learn that every thought is not to be spoken. You must also learn to master your mouth. There are going to be times when you want to get your point across even after the conversation or disagreement has ended. You are going to have to learn how to shut your mouth, swallow your pride and keep it moving.

Remember, to keep yourself girded up in strength and to always walk in integrity. Remember the dream. Do not allow people to take you out of character. Each time someone tries to take you out of character, remember the dream. Remember the road that you have already traveled to get to the point you are at now. Remember all that you have accomplished and what more lies ahead. In all in all remember who you are.

Always remember that change starts with you. You may not be able to change others perspective about you, but you can change you. You can adapt your behaviors for where you are going. It's all about the dream. Keep the dream before you day in and day out. Keep the dream in your heart, your mind and in eyesight.

Having dreams allow you to overlook so many things that really do not matter. Having dreams allow you to look over the minor and concentrate on the major, goal, and the objective. Someone asked was winning the outcome? My answer was Yes. Yes, because you will fail so many times that when you taste the victory of a win it will be a feeling like no other. So Yes, win and do not stop. Because you will taste enough failures. To win you will fail so many times, but those are learning experiences. Keep your eyes on the prize and keep it moving until you reach the goal line. You can succeed in this life and you can create and build a very successful business, but it all starts with a dream.

Pointers in It All Starts With A Dream:

1. Surround yourself around people who want to see you win
2. Research, study and learn from mentors
3. Change starts with you
4. You must have a plan
5. You must allow Faith to be activated
6. Count the cost
7. Success does not happen overnight
8. You got to put the work in
9. You must master you
10. Do not listen to negativity or negative people

(Chapters I-III Questionnaire & Activity)

1. When you look in the mirror what do you see?

___

___

___

___

___

___

___

2. What insecurities you deal with that you feel are stopping you from moving forward?

___

___

___

___

___

___

___

3. Do you believe facing your fears is important and if so why?

____

____

____

____

____

____

____

____

4. What giants in your life you feel you must conquer to succeed?

____

____

____

____

____

____

____

5. What childhood issue you are still dealing with and feel is stopping you from becoming all that you know you could be?

____

____

____

____

____

____

____

6. What does the word mentor mean to you? And do you feel mentor are needed?

____

____

____

____

____

____

____

7. Why is it important to master your emotions, your opinions and your mouth?

____

____

____

____

____

____

____

____

8. How long have you been on the road to discovery?

____

____

____

____

____

____

____

____

9. Why is it important to be honest and upfront and real about who you are?

____

____

____

____

____

____

____

10. What do you think about chapters 1-3? And do you see yourself in these chapters and if so, what would you improve?

____

____

____

____

____

____

____

CHAPTER IV

No is Not the Final Answer

While you are building and working towards your dreams, you are going to encounter some No's, but do not be dismayed or discouraged. Keep going; keep asking; keep building until you hear a Yes. Challenges come when you are working on dreams, but do not allow the challenges to overtake you. You must be so solid in your belief that when you hear a No, you are not shaken, but it convinces you more than ever that what you are building is something great.

Let me take some time and encourage you a little. I want you to know that you are and were not the first person to hear No. If you research several success stories you will find that the very person and or people that you admire have heard the word No more than twenty times before they finally got a Yes.

When you hear No, it just means that your faith is being tested, and you got to ask yourself, "how bad do I want this". If you want this dream to come to pass bad enough, you will keep trying until you hear Yes, because No, is never the final answer. Especially when you are building.

I would not be telling you the truth if I told you that things are gong to run smoothly and that you are just going to walk into the banks and or investors are going to jump on your ship right away. I would not be telling you the truth if I told you that it will be easy, and people will just hand you millions of dollars to complete your project. Yes, I believe in faith. Yes, I believe in miracles, but one thing for sure, I know that miracles happen after we do something, and that is after we persevere.

Persevering all the way to the end. All the way until we hear Yes. I am reminded of how many times Thomas Edison failed before he finally accomplished his dream of developing electric power generations, mass communication and sound recording. He failed many times, but he kept inventing. He kept going until he saw a Yes.

You must look at your No's as opportunities not rejections. In reading some of Edison's quotes you will see why he finally succeeded. It was his (Thomas Edison's) mindset:

1. "I have not failed. I've just found 10,000 ways that won't work". (Thomas Edison)

2. "Our greatest weakness lies in giving up. The most certain way to succeed is always to try just one more time". (Thomas Edison)
3. "There's a way to do it better-find it" (Thomas Edison)
4. "Many of life's failures are people who did not realize how close they were to success when they gave up". (Thomas Edison) www.brainyquotes.com

There were so many other inventors that refused to take No for an answer. I can name so many people who have passed and many who are still living and enjoying the fruits of their labor. They all will tell you that before their name became great, people were just walking by them as if they were transparent.

To Be Your Best Self Yet, you are going to have to learn how to keep going when no one knows your name. I am reminded of another inventor. The first woman ever in the U.S. history to become a self-made millionaire, who built an empire from absolutely nothing, her birth name was Sarah Breedlove, who is known by the world as Madam C.J. Walker. She burst through many glass ceilings as she heard No several times but kept on going. (Henry Louis Gates, Jr. Time Magazine 12/7/98)

Just as Madam C.J. Walker built her fortune from nothing, and kept on pioneering, you can build yours too. You must have a made-up mind, a will to win, and a dream worth fighting for.

Yes, dreams are worth fighting for. And if your dream is worth fighting for, you will win. You will not take No for an answer. You will push until a door opens. You will pull until all your fears come tumbling down. You will keep on going until you no longer hear the words No, but Yes.

When you are at your weakest is when you are to press on even harder. Imagine going through heart-ache and pain, rejection after rejection, experiencing let downs, and because of pressure, you give up. How would you feel if you found out that you gave up, and you were just one hour away from total victory? How would you feel? All that hard work and time you put into that dream. All those late nights you stayed awake and sacrifices you made, to give up right at the point of victory would make you a very disheartened person.

If that is you I am talking to, and you have given up, I want to encourage you to get your focus back. You are not the only person who stopped. And certainly, will not be the last. You just rested for a while. The difference between a person who stopped and a person who quits is obvious. The person who stopped only rested for a while; however, the person who quits gave it all up and walked away. But you are not a quitter. You are a winner. And for sure, you will win.

You who are reading this book, I want you to know that It is time for you to get your focus back. It is time to reposition yourself to win. You just stopped to regain strength, I understand. You just stopped to get your plan in order, and now it is time for you to walk again. Yes, walk again. Get back on the road to destiny. Get back on the road to fulfilling your dreams.

I have faith in you. You will probably hear several other No's, but do not allow that to put you in a place of dismay. Now that you have regained your focus, you got to learn how to master the No. You got to learn how to let the No's slide off your back and not look at them again. It is a reason I said, slide off your back. The reason being is because every No that you have received, is behind you now. That's right, it is how you look at it. It is how you think of it. Remember, earlier on we talked about how Thomas Edison and Madam C.J. Walker had the mindsets to keep on going despite? That is the same mind-set you are going to have to put on. Despite all disappointments, I am going on. And this time, I am not stopping.

To encourage you, I want you to remember these great people who did not quit after hardship:

1. If Steve Jobs had never been fired, he would not have brought Pixar and turned out Apple after he got back to the company.

2. Remember, Walt Disney? Had he not been fired form the newspaper company for what they said was his "lack of imagination", we would not be taking out children to Disney World or Disney Land.
3. Also, do not let age get in the way. Remember Colonel Sanders? He had a restaurant before KFC that did not do well, had he quit after the restaurant went out of business, there would be no KFC. Shawn Lim www.stunningmotivation.com

So, you see? Everyone who went on to be great suffered No's. Success did not come without a No, or several No's. However, these successful people did not allow the No's to overtake them to the point of destruction. They used their "set- backs as set-ups for comebacks". Willey Jolley, 10/12/99. And in the end, they won, and won big. You can win too. You must keep going until you reach the goal line. Keep going until you reach the end. And it is only the end when you win.

Now that you got the motivation to keep going it is important to know that you will hear No again. Some of the things you can do when you hear No is to go back and look at your business plan. Ask yourself if you need to adjust some things or do you need to make some minor adjustments. Maybe you received a No because of your speech. Record yourself speaking and listen attentively to hear if you are using certain words to much. I know that sometimes I find myself using the words "um or you know what I am saying", an awful lot. Another thing you may want to do is practice your presentation skills in front of some very harsh critics and listen to the adjustments and or advice they may provide.

Remember, there is nothing wrong with adjusting the plan and or improving ourselves. We started this book off with always continue to learn. Always continue to get counsel and guidance, and always ask questions. No one made it to the top all by themselves. They had mentors and counselors and teachers to help guide them through the process.

One thing I want you to know, that which comes great success, comes a grueling process. If you want to be mediocre then you will still go through a process, but if you want to be a world changer, and have great success, you will go through a grueling process. You may be asking yourself, "why does it have to be grueling"? Well, one of the reasons is greatness does not happen over-night. Even if you were born with greatness in you, you would need to discover it, cultivate it, and then act upon it.

Yes, some people can be taught to be great. I do believe people can be taught anything. They can be taught to be good or evil. They can be taught to be rich or stay in poverty. That is why it is important to have the mindset to be great. Because having the mindset, will and determination rest upon the one who is trying to do the accomplishing.

As a coach I can motivate you all day long. I can send you encouraging messages. I can send you emails throughout the day with positive quotes. I can send you website links to read articles on success stories; however, if you do not get up and use what was given to you, nothing would come out of it.

That is why it is important that you know who you are. You will find that many people will make assumptions about you. People will make perceptions about you. And people will try to tell you who you are based on their limited view of you or based on what others have said about you. They will even try to define you and try to talk you out of your dream. You must be unmovable, unshakeable, unbreakable and unstoppable.

Being firm in your convictions. Because some of the people that you are looking to get a Yes from, will be the very ones weary of you. Remember to keep going until you hear a Yes, because No is not the final answer.

Pointers for No Is Not the Final Answer:

1. Do not be dismayed or discouraged when you hear a No
2. When you are at your weakest is when you are to press even harder
3. If you need to adjust your plan do so
4. If you need to practice your presentation skills do so
5. It is okay for you to stop, but not okay for you to quit
6. Persevere until you hear a Yes
7. Know who you are
8. You must have the mindset to be great
9. Read success stories of others
10. Be firm in your convictions.

CHAPTER V

Conquer Your Mountain

While you're building and moving forward with your plans you will find that you will encounter some situations, issues and circumstances that can look like mountains. And no matter how hard you pushed, pressed or pulled, that situation, issue or circumstance refused to move. In those instances, you are going to have to learn other avenues to conquer those mountains. They are not moving. They are not disappearing. They are at a standstill. In short, some mountains you're going to have to climb.

Yes, it easy to dodge the mountains and some you can. It is also easier to find other routes. However, to get to the other side of a specific issue, it is going to cause you to go through a process. And the process may feel like you are climbing up a mountain. But let me assure you that the process is preparing you for the reach, and the reach is preparing you for the grab.

In life we all must go through processes to become great. And the closer you get to fulfilling the dream the harder the process may seem to be getting. This stage is simply called your mountain experience. In this process you are going to experience excitement and anxiety due to almost completing what you have started. In the next phase of the process you are going to experience adversity and exertion, due to seeing the fulfillment of the dream, but not yet able to grab hold of it.

The word "through" in the process phase is important for you to maintain in your memory when you are in your mountain experience. Holding on to the word "through" keeps you determined to climb no matter what because there is something waiting for you on the other side of that mountain. And you are going to climb and conquer that mountain without fail.

While you are climbing, remember all those you look up to and consider great, had to climb to get to the top. Greatness just wasn't handed to them. When I think about the process towards greatness, I like to consider the Butterfly and the Ant. I believe both species are fantastic as it relates to their process and preparation to greatness.

When you study the butterfly, it humbles you and gives you a fresh perspective about your own process. As you look at the butterfly flying, and all the different colors that are represented, you think, there is no way something this beautiful can come out of something as slimy, ugly and crawly as the caterpillar.

Yes, before the butterfly was beautiful in all its glory, it once was known as a caterpillar in which some would say is not good to look upon at all. The butterfly goes through what is called a metamorphosis. To be considered an adult the butterfly must go through 4 stages: egg, larva, pupa and adult. Let's explore the butterfly a little more, because as the butterfly goes through its stages, you too must go through stages and or processes to be considered Your Best Self Yet.

The egg stage consists of the butterfly starting life as an oval looking egg. Their eggs are laid on leaves or plants. Some eggs are round, and some eggs are oval shaped. Just as you are different than any other person in life, and the road you must travel to destiny and promise, and or to dream fulfillment is different than any other person; The butterfly is the same. There are different type of butterflies and depending on the type of butterfly depends on the type of egg that would be laid.

When the butterfly egg hatches the larvae, the second stage, which is considered the caterpillar, is formed or considered born. The caterpillar must eat to grow. And in this stage, they mainly eat. As the caterpillar eats, it grows by what is called "molting" (shedding the outgrown skin). This process occurs several times throughout the larvae stage.

The third stage is called the Pupa. As soon as the butterfly stops growing and they have reached maturity, which consists of their full length and weight, they are formed into what is called the Pupa. If you look on the outside of the Pupa you may think the caterpillar is dead or sleeping, because it looks like it is not moving. However, the inside is where all the changes are being made, and the caterpillar is rapidly changing.

If you look at the Pupa stage, that is what happens to you as you are growing. When you are faced with mountains and trials in life, sometimes it feels like you are not growing or that you are in the same place. However, something on the inside of you is changing. You are gaining more strength. Your faith is growing. Your determination deepens. Your passion to win and to succeed grows, and most of all you are being prepared to manage, oversee and preside over that which is on the other side of that mountain.

When the Pupa stage has been completed, the caterpillar's tissues, limbs, and organs all have been changed and is ready for what is the final stage, and that is called the Adult Butterfly.

The butterfly emerges with both wings folded against the body. Blood is pumped through the wings to get the wings to function properly. And that is when we see the beautiful butterfly stretching its wings to fly.

Just like that, but not really. What I mean by not really is that the process did not happen overnight. And whether you are working on a business or working on bettering yourself, it will not happen overnight. There is a process to the madness of it all. And through the pain the rain, the heartache and many times not understanding, it is important to submit to the process of you becoming Your Best Self Yet.

I would like to also compare you to the life of the Ant. Why did I choose the Ant? I chose the Ant because the Ant is one of the wisest of its species. I say this because they are small but have the sense to know when to prepare.

The Ant is masterful when it comes to preparing. Ants see their mountains and do not wait until they get close to the mountain to try to find a way to climb. They prepare for what is ahead. Ants are not strong in stature, but they are strong in work ethic. They are hardworking and very productive and are known for building great structures. They are known to prepare for the future, and they are known to be very successful in ensuring their families are taken care of throughout the Winter months. Many things can be learned from looking at the Ant's work ethic.

1. The Ant prepared for what is ahead
2. The Ant is not easily distracted.
3. The Ant does not operate in procrastination.
4. The Ant is extremely focused.
5. The Ant is self-motivated.

These things are important to point out. If these 5 strategies are planned out in your life, I am sure without a doubt you will be able to conquer your mountain. Always remember that preparation is the key to winning. Prepare for the days ahead. Always count the cost. Come up with strategies ahead of time to help problem-solve and deal with any surprising issues. Write down a road map in case you must revise your plan and take another route. Always be ready to change course if needed, meaning not allowing change to put you in a state of fear, but meeting change with stamina and strength.

When building and working on yourself it is important to let go of people, places and things that bring on distraction. Do not let in anything or anyone that will cause you to take your mind off the goal at hand. And that is to climb and conquer that mountain. Distraction can cause someone to come along clip you up or throw you off YOUR mountain.

Do not allow procrastination to set in. Procrastination will stop progress, and you would look back, ten years later, and find you are still at the bottom of the mountain waiting for someone to help you up. Procrastination is a killer. It is not your friend. And its goal is to steal your passion and your confidence. It wants to steal your desires and destroy your vision.

The goal is to stay focused. You have a mountain to climb and to conquer; therefore, you do not have time to be looking at someone else, and what they are doing. Keep your focus on climbing the mountain that you have been purposed to climb and conquer, or else you will fall.

Allow self-motivation to become your best friend. No one will be on that mountain with you. You are going to have to motivate and encourage yourself all the way up to the top and over. You are going to have to speak to legs and command your legs not to get tired. You are going to have to command your mind to stay focused. You are going to have to command your ears to hear yourself speaking words of life and not death. You are going to have to command your eyes to see the word winner.

If the caterpillar can allow itself to go through the process to bloom into a beautiful butterfly, so can you go through the process to bloom into a beautiful, accomplished, successful version of Your Best Self Yet.

If the Ant can prepare for its future so that it will not fail or starve, so can you prepare for your future so that you will not fail or starve. Preparation has never led anyone down the wrong road or mountain; therefore, prepare yourself for every mountain you must face. Prepare yourself for every mountain you must climb. And prepare yourself to go over to the other side and reach for your dreams. Reach for your promise. Reach for the new you and celebrate becoming Your Best Self Yet.

Pointers To Conquer Your Mountain

1. Do not dodge the mountain; conquer the mountain.
2. It is okay to go through your process.
3. Take notes from the Caterpillar formed Butterfly.
4. Do not fight the process.
5. Take notes from the life of the Ant.
6. Prepare
7. Do not become distracted
8. Do not procrastinate
9. Stay Focused
10. Self-Motivate

CHAPTER VI

REACH OUT AND GRAB IT

After the process comes the prize. The very thing that you have been working for is now in eyesight. And all you must do at this very moment is reach out and grab it. You are ready to climb your mountain. The process has come to an end and you have finally made up in your mind that you are going up and over. As you climb do not look down. Do not look back. Do not look to the right or to the left but keep looking up. Keep looking toward the finish line.

On the other side of that mountain is your prize. The only thing standing between you and your promise, dream or goal is you. Your thoughts will determine if you go over to the other side. Remember, as you climb to think on good things, think on positive things, and think on things that would help motivate you to continue the climb.

So many people want to take the easy way out but remember the closer you get to the finish line is when it feels the bumpiest and the hardest. If you keep going and hold on to the rough edges, you will surely prevail.

If you are wondering why the side of the mountain you are climbing is so rough, let me assure you it is needed for you to go over. Do not worry about the rough side of the mountain. You are on the right side. The rough side is needed so that you can hold on. The rough side is needed to help hold your weight. The rough side is needed to help hold your balance.

For it is the soft side that will cause you to fall. That side of the mountain is the easy way out and will cause you to tumble. That side of the mountain seams easy, with no lumps or bumps, but do not be deceived because it is the side that would cause you slip. And anything that would cause you slip is the thing that you want to avoid.

The soft side of the mountain causes the fall because it does not challenge you. The soft side of the mountain causes tumbles because it does not leave room for steadiness. The soft side of the mountain causes slips because it is not strong enough to grip you into the position you need to be to keep climbing to the top.

Holding on to the rough side of the mountain is pivotal for your climb. It teaches you to never let go of your dreams even when it feels too hard to hold on to them. Even when your hands feel like letting go, the rough side of the mountain talks back to you and tells you if you let go now you will die. Yes, not a physical death, but one that eats at your soul and repeatedly speaks to you, torments you, and tells you that you have come too far let go now.

Climbing the rough side of the mountain is needed to hold your weight. That's right, everything was not made to carry you. Your dreams are so heavy and so dense that it takes the rough side of the mountain to sustain the gravity of the weight of them. Therefore, you need to keep holding on to the rough edges so that they can continue to hold your weight.

And finally, the rough side is needed to hold your balance. This side of the mountain keeps you balanced. Many times, while climbing, you cried. However, many times you also laughed. Many times, while climbing you felt pain. However, many times you also felt joy.

Having a balanced mindset helped you to defeat every doubt. It helped you to defeat antagonism. It also helped you to see the bright side of situations and circumstances. The rough side of the mountain helped you pass tests and taught you how to persevere and endure.

So many people want to take the easy way out but remember the closer you get to the finish line is when it feels the bumpiest and the hardest. If you keep going and hold on to the rough edges, you will surely prevail.

You will get to the top of that mountain and eventually on the other side.

Hardship is inevitable when building your dreams and passions. However, the rough side of the mountain allows those things that seemed impossible to become possible. I believe in your dream and passions. You will taste victory and will be able to look back and proclaim it was worth it all.

You have climbed through the rain. You have climbed through the pain. You have climbed through the frustrations and disappointments. And now it is time for you to simply reach out and grab it. There is nothing stopping you from grabbing hold to that promise or to that dream. It is within you reach.

Some things in life you are going to have to grab. You are going to have to snatch. Poverty does not want to leave your life and it will fight you tooth and nail; but you got to make up in your mind that if you must reach out and grab your dream, you will.

It is your dream. You worked hard for that business. You worked hard for that vision to come to pass, and this is not the time to be passive. This is the time to be aggressive and go all out. You have just climbed up a few mountains to reach your goal, and now that it is within your reach, you must be aggressive and grab and snatch it, and whatever else it takes to keep it because it belongs to you.

In your aggressive stage, which in this instance, is the reach out and grab it stage, you must continue to build upon what has been established. Aggressive is not a bad word. There is nothing wrong with going after what you want. And in many cases, you must go hard and be unmovable and unstoppable. To continue to build and be Your Best Self Yet, here are a list of things that you **must not** allow to occur.

1. The stopping of celebrations. Complacency and Comfortability.
2. A dim perspective and outlook.
3. Lack to change and or adjust and revise your business plan.
4. Stop Networking with other winners.
5. Stop setting new goals.

What do I mean by do not stop celebrating? Many times, when people reach their goals they become comfortable and complacent. However, if you want to continue to be Your Best Self, you must be consistent in your method of winning. Do not stop celebrating. Consistency is the key to a very successful life; however, complacency and comfortability only makes one slothful. Therefore, you must continue to celebrate. Celebrate your victories. Celebrate your milestones. Celebrate those who have journeyed with you. And most of all celebrate you.

Do not allow negative perspectives or dim outlooks on situations to take over. You have defeated these things while going through your process and anything else that stayed after the process, was drained while climbing the mountain. Remember negativity will only stunt your growth.

Negativity will kill any dream. And will stop fruitfulness. Negativity can stop progress and keep you from making crucial decisions that will impact your future. Dim outlooks already tell your environment that it is doomed. Therefore, you want to stay away from dim outlooks. Remember, your words hold power.

Do not allow a lack to change or adapt to new skills, abilities, or processes keep you stagnant. Change is inevitable. Being open and able to adapt to new possibilities is a great personal and business skill. Change is not always bad. In fact, change is very good. In a world that is always changing, if you do not change with the times, you will get left behind.

At anytime always revise your business plan to fit the needs of the structure. Adapting and not being afraid to chart out new goals is crucial to your success as a business owner or even working on your own personal self-goals.

Do not ever stop networking. Remember, your connections are vital to keeping your success. Do not get prideful. Always walk in humility; for you should know better than anyone, especially after having to climb those mountains, the importance of connections. In any relationship, whether it is business, personal or work related, that staying connected is crucial for continued success. Some very important benefits networking will do for you:

1. Networking will keep a flow of prospects coming your way.
2. Networking will help you exchange new and fresh ideas.
3. Networking will allow you to offer your services to others.
4. Networking will open of new doors of opportunity for you.
5. Networking will expand your influence.

Do not ever stop setting new goals. Only a fool stops growing. Remember, growth is very necessary. It is necessary for you to be Your Best Self Yet, as well for your business to prosper.

1. Goals will allow you to stay focused and on course.
2. Goals help you to get maximum results.
3. Goals help you be the best you can be.

Therefore, continue to write them down and speak them out loud until you see the manifestation of them in your life. Because those goals will see you through triumphs and will help you reach out and grab your dreams with love and passion.

At this point, staying focused and on course should not be hard for you. You have climbed the hardest mountain there is, fought through the toughest trial and have endured bumps and potholes while walking on your road to discovery. You have accomplished and overcame all of this and you are still standing. That alone is something to celebrate and be happy about.

There is no reason to look back at the past. You have reached the top, and the goal now is to stay at the top. You have won, and the goal is to keep winning. You have succeeded, and the goal now is to continue to succeed. You reached out and you grabbed your dream, and now it is time for you to keep moving forward. It is time for you to keep looking ahead. It is time for you to expand your horizons and enlarge your territory. It is time for you to help someone else become their Best Self Yet because it is all about giving back.

The only time you should look back and to reach back is to help someone else through the dirty potholed roads, steep hills and rough mountains, you once had to climb. You have accomplished much just by persevering, shattering glass ceilings, stretching boundaries and removing barriers. You reached, and you grabbed it. You are at the height of your awareness and ready to live Your Best Self Yet.

Pointers To Reach and Grab It

1. You are the only person that can stand between your dream and goal.
2. The rough side of the mountain is needed.
3. Do not look back at your past.
4. Never stop setting goals.
5. Continue to network.
6. Look back only to reach back to help someone else.
7. Negativity will kill your dreams.
8. Always walk in humility.
9. Continue to celebrate victories.
10. Be aggressive about winning.

Chapters IV-VI Questionnaire & Activity

1. Have you ever experienced a closed door that was a for sure No?

____

____

____

____

____

____

____

2. How did the No make you feel?

____

____

____

____

____

____

3. Have you ever felt like quitting and if so what stopped you?

____

____

____

____

____

____

____

____

4. Do you see your life in the caterpillar or the ant? Explain.

____

____

____

____

____

____

____

5. In order to complete your goals what distractions you had to let go?

____

____

____

____

____

____

____

____

6. What mountains (hardships) you have had to overcome?

____

____

____

____

____

____

____

7. Why is it important to continue even if you feel like quitting?

8. Which side of the mountain would you prefer? The rough or soft side?

9. What is your definition of aggressive? Do you believe there is something wrong with being aggressive?

____

____

____

____

____

____

____

10. What is the absolute best part of chapters I-VI that you find yourself?

____

____

____

____

____

____

____

CHAPTER VII

YOUR BEST SELF YET-CLOSING

The road to unlocking the greatness that's inside of you can be long. Your experiences helped shape, develop and prepare you for your destination. I started this book off with pointing out the importance of self-discovery. And the different phases and stages you would go through before you reach your dreams.

Self-discovery is one of the upmost important factors because if you do not know who you are you will be bounced and tossed here and there, marching to the sound of everyone's orders, but your own.

Facing your fears will play a factor in you completing your assignments. There will be many situations and circumstances that will arise; however, if you are not able to face the fears within, you will not be able to face the fears without. Fears are there to trick you out of your destiny. Fear robs you of your potential. However, renouncing it and refusing to succumb to your fears will lead you to higher and greater heights in life.

It all starts with a dream. Yes, before you can begin you must have a dream. You must have a vision for beginning. It is the dream that will keep you motivated. It is the dream that will keep you encouraged. It is the dream that will keep you when you feel like giving up. It is the dream that will help you complete what it is that you started.

In life you are going to encounter many No's, but you must keep knocking until you hear a Yes. No is not uncommon when you are building and working toward fulfilling your dream. No is not uncommon but is very common. You must keep going even if you must knock down some doors to get a Yes. Be rest assured in knowing that No is not the final answer.

Barriers and obstacles will come your way, but you got to keep plowing until you conquer your mountain. Some mountains you will be able to speak to and they will disappear, but there are just some mountains you are going to have to climb. You are going to have to climb in your rainy seasons of life. You are going to have to climb in your dry seasons of life, and you are going to have to climb in your lonely seasons of life. Whatever you do, just don't stop climbing.

After the Climb, there shall be glory. Glory that you have finally made it. Glory that you did it. Glory that you have won. Glory that you have completed the goal. And Glory that you conquered your mountain.

Do not get stuck and complacent on the win. Continue to reach out and grab everything that your heart desires. It is yours for the taking. You have sweated. You have lost sleep. You have lost love ones. You have been misunderstood. You have sacrificed more than enough. And now all you must do is reach out and grab it.

I want to write you a letter, and in this letter, I want you to know how proud I am of you. I am proud of the person you have become. I am proud that you did not allow yourself to become a negative statistic. I am proud that you did not allow your negative environment to cause you to slumber. I am proud that you broke from the crowds. I am proud that you kept going when everyone else stopped. I am proud that you won.

I celebrate and rejoice with you in all your victories because I know they did not come easy. Life is not easy, and it takes a strong person to defeat it. Life has not defeated you; You have defeated life. I celebrate you because I understand your sacrifices. I celebrate with you because I understand your road. I celebrate with you because I know your heart. I know that with everything within you, you wanted to win, and you did. However, most importantly, you did not compromise your integrity to do it. You won, and you won fair and square.

I end this letter with encouragement and motivation. I want you to know that you are Your Best Self. Some days you will not feel like your Best Self, but you got to speak to your mind and your heart and command them to agree with your purpose, the plan and the promise.

You have won, but there will be many other opportunities and times to win again. I just say continue. You have mastered one thing that has built your foundation. That one thing is YOU. You have mastered you. You have searched deep within to discover the gold and treasure inside. You have conquered fears and climbed mountains. And now it is time for you to simply, SHINE.

Shine so bright my beautiful STAR. Shine so bright that the other stars will have to concede. Shine through the rain. Shine through the pain. Shine through the curtains, Yes, the curtains. Many will try to cover you up, but you got to keep on shining. Shine so bright that when they try to place the covers over you, your brightness will overshadow them.

Greatness can't be stopped. Greatness is not a mistake. Greatness can't be moved. Greatness can't lose. At the end of the day, greatness wins every time. So, my beautiful bright shining star. Yes, you are the greatest out of all the stars in the galaxy. Keep being great and don't lose your shine, simply remain Your Best Self Yet!

I AM Declaration

I AM Beautiful
I AM Unique
I AM Gifted
I AM Wonderfully Made
I AM Courageous
I AM Able
I AM Determined
I AM Focused
I AM Intelligent
I AM Knowledgeable
I AM Articulate
I AM Successful
I AM Prosperous
I AM Abundant
I AM Fruitful
I AM Complete
I AM Healed
I AM Happy
I AM Wealthy
I AM Bodacious
I AM
I AM My Best Self Yet

I See You Decree

I See You Successful

I See You Prosperous

I See You Healthy

I See You Winning

I See You Breaking Barriers

I See You Changing the World

I See You Breaking Glass Ceilings

I See You Building Businesses All Over the World

I See You Leaving An Inheritance For Your Children and Their Children

I See You Helping Others

I See You Mentoring Others

I See You Coaching Others

I See You With An Overflow of Blessings

I See You Leading Nations

I See You Loving Yourself and Others

I see You Forgiving Yourself and Others

I See You With Manifested Blessings

I See You With Multiple Streams of Income

I See You With Long-Life

I See You Wealthy

I See You Finishing Every Project Started

I See You Your Best Self Yet

Motivational Quotes

1. Our greatest glory is not in never falling, but in rising every time we fall. — Confucius
2. All our dreams can come true, if we have the courage to pursue them. – Walt Disney
3. It does not matter how slowly you go as long as you do not stop. – Confucius
4. Everything you've ever wanted is on the other side of fear. — George Addair
5. Hardships often prepare ordinary people for an extraordinary destiny. – C.S. Lewis
6. Believe in yourself. You are braver than you think, more talented than you know, and capable of more than you imagine. — Roy T. Bennett
7. I learned that courage was not the absence of fear, but the triumph over it. The brave man is not he who does not feel afraid, but he who conquers that fear. – Nelson Mandela
8. There is only one thing that makes a dream impossible to achieve: the fear of failure. — Paulo Coelho

9. Your true success in life begins only when you make the commitment to become excellent at what you do. — Brian Tracy
10. Believe in yourself, take on your challenges, dig deep within yourself to conquer fears. Never let anyone bring you down. You got to keep going. – Chantal Sutherland
11. If you set goals and go after them with all the determination you can muster, your gifts will take you places that will amaze you. – Les Brown
12. Hard times don't create heroes. It is during the hard times when the 'hero' within us is revealed. – Bob Riley
13. Most of the important things in the world have been accomplished by people who have kept on trying when there seemed to be no hope at all. — Dale Carnegie
14. Don't be pushed around by the fears in your mind. Be led by the dreams in your heart. — Roy T. Bennett
15. You're going to go through tough times – that's life. But I say, 'Nothing happens to you, it happens for you.' See the positive in negative events. – Joel Osteen
16. Character cannot be developed in ease and quiet. Only through experience of trial and suffering

can the soul be strengthened, ambition inspired, and success achieved. – Helen Keller

17. It's not about perfect. It's about effort. And when you bring that effort every single day, that's where transformation happens. That's how change occurs. – Jillian Michaels
18. Learn from the past, set vivid, detailed goals for the future, and live in the only moment of time over which you have any control: now. – Denis Waitley
19. If you don't like something, change it. If you can't change it, change your attitude. – Maya Angelou
20. Failure will never overtake me if my determination to succeed is strong enough. – Og Mandino
21. Inaction breeds doubt and fear. Action breeds confidence and courage. If you want to conquer fear, do not sit home and think about it. Go out and get busy. – Dale Carnegie
22. Inaction breeds doubt and fear. Action breeds confidence and courage. If you want to conquer fear, do not sit home and think about it. Go out and get busy. – Dale Carnegie
23. Inaction breeds doubt and fear. Action breeds confidence and courage. If you want to conquer fear, do not sit home and think about it. Go out and get busy. – Dale Carnegie

24. **Believe in yourself! Have faith in your abilities! Without a humble but reasonable confidence in your own powers you cannot be successful or happy. – Norman Vincent Peale**
25. **Your time is limited, so don't waste it living someone else's life. – Steve Jobs**
26. **Challenges are what make life interesting and overcoming them is what makes life meaningful. – Joshua Marine**
27. **You cannot afford to live in potential for the rest of your life; at some point, you must unleash the potential and make your move. – Eric Thomas**
28. **There is no greater disability in society than the inability to see a person as more. – Robert M. Hensel**
29. **The Secret of Change Is to Focus All of Your Energy, Not on Fighting the Old, But on Building the New – Socrates**
30. **The greatest danger for most of us is not that our aim is too high and we miss it, but that it is too low and we reach it. – Michaelangelo**
31. **The two most important days in your life are the day you are born and the day you find out why. – Mark Twain**
32. **"Courage doesn't happen when you have all the answers. It happens when you are ready to face**

the questions you have been avoiding your whole life." — Shannon L. Alder

33. "Work like there is someone else working twenty-four hours a day to take it away from you." – Mark Cuban
34. "When you know what you want, and want it bad enough, you'll find a way to get it." – Jim Rohn
35. "To conquer frustration, one must remain intensely focused on the outcome, not the obstacles." — T.F. Hodge

ENCOURAGEMENT QUOTES

1. "Everyone has inside them a piece of good news. The good news is you don't know how great you can be! How much you can love! What you can accomplish! And what your potential is." – Anne Frank
2. "Don't think, just do." – Horace
3. "Expect problems and eat them for breakfast." – Alfred A. Montapert
4. "You just can't beat the person who never gives up." – Babe Ruth
5. "The harder the conflict, the more glorious the triumph." – Thomas Paine
6. "The first step toward success is taken when you refuse to be a captive of the environment in which you first find yourself." – Mark Caine
7. "Start where you are. Use what you have. Do what you can." – Arthur Ashe
8. "Set your goals high, and don't stop till you get there." – Bo Jackson
9. "Either you run the day or the day runs you." – Jim Rohn

10. "In order to succeed, we must first believe that we can." – Nikos Kazantzakis
11. "Always do your best. What you plant now, you will harvest later." – Og Mandino
12. "A man can be as great as he wants to be. If you believe in yourself and have the courage, the determination, the dedication, the competitive drive and if you are willing to sacrifice the little things in life and pay the price for the things that are worthwhile, it can be done." – Vince Lombardi
13. "Do you want to know who you are? Don't ask. Act! Action will delineate and define you." – Thomas Jefferson
14. "Character cannot be developed in ease and quiet. Only through experience of trial and suffering can the soul be strengthened, ambition inspired, and success achieved." – Hellen Keller
15. "It is very important to know who you are. To make decisions. To show who you are." – Malala Yousafzai
16. "Never complain and never explain." – Benjamin Disraeli
17. "We may encounter many defeats, but we must not be defeated." – Maya Angelou

18. "Our greatest weakness lies in giving up. The most certain way to succeed is always to try just one more time." – Thomas A. Edison
19. "You will never do anything in this world without courage. It is the greatest quality in the mind next to honor." – Aristotle
20. "True happiness involves the full use of one's power and talents." – John W. Gardner
21. "Even if you fall on your face, you're still moving forward." – Victor Kiam
22. "Press on – nothing can take the place of persistence. Talent will not; nothing is more common than unsuccessful men with talent. Genius will not; unrewarded genius is almost a proverb. Education will not; the world is full of educated derelicts. Perseverance and determination alone are omnipotent." – Calvin Coolidge
23. "Be miserable. Or motivate yourself. Whatever has to be done, it's always your choice." – Wayne Dyer
24. "Often we women are risk averse. I needed the push. Now, more than ever, young women need more seasoned women to provide that encouragement, to take a risk, to go for it. Once a glass ceiling is broken, it stays broken." – Jennifer Grahnolm

25. "When one door closes another door opens; but we so often look so long and so regretfully upon the closed door, that we do not see the ones which open for us." – Alexander Graham Bell
26. "Quality is not an act, it is a habit." – Aristotle
27. "Life is a succession of lessons which must be lived to be understood." – Helen Keller
28. "Accept the challenges so that you can feel the exhilaration of victory." – George S. Patton
29. "I decided, very early on, just to accept life unconditionally; I never expected it to do anything special for me, yet I seemed to accomplish far more than I had ever hoped. Most of the time it just happened to me without my ever seeking it." – Audrey Hepburn
30. "You must do the thing you think you cannot do." – Eleanor Roosevelt
31. ", if we want to direct our lives, we must take control of our consistent actions. It's not what we do once in a while that shapes our lives, but what we do consistently." – Tony Robbins
32. "When life knocks you down, try to land on your back. Because if you can look up, you can get up." – Les Brown
33. "Somehow I can't believe that there are any heights that can't be scaled by a man who

knows the secrets of making dreams come true. This special secret, it seems to me, can be summarized in four C s. They are curiosity, confidence, courage, and constancy, and the greatest of all is confidence. When you believe in a thing, believe in it all the way, implicitly and unquestionable." – Walt Disney

SUCCESS QUOTES

1. The only true wisdom is knowing that you know nothing." Socrates
2. "Things work out best for those who make the best of how things work out." John Wooden
3. "Let no feeling of discouragement prey upon you, and in the end, you are sure to succeed." Abraham Lincoln
4. "If you are not willing to risk the usual you will have to settle for the ordinary." Jim Rohn
5. "Innovation distinguishes between a leader and a follower." Steve Jobs
6. "The more you lose yourself in something bigger than yourself, the more energy you will have." Norman Vincent Peale
7. "If your ship doesn't come in, swim out to meet it!" Jonathan Winters
8. "People often say that motivation doesn't last. Well, neither does bathing – that's why we recommend it daily." Zig Ziglar
9. "Courage is being scared to death but saddling up anyway." John Wayne

10. **"Too many of us are not living our dreams because we are living our fears." Les Brown**
11. **"The link between my experience as an entrepreneur and that of a politician is all in one word: freedom." Silvio Berlusconi**
12. **"The entrepreneur builds an enterprise; the technician builds a job." Michael Gerber**

Success Stories

1. **Arianna Huffington got rejected by 36 publishers.** It's hard to believe that one of the most recognizable names in online publications was once rejected by three dozen major publishers. Huffington's second book, which she tried to publish long before she created the now ubiquitously recognizable Huffington Post empire, was rejected 36 times before it was eventually accepted for publication.

   Even Huffington Post itself wasn't a success right away. In fact, when it launched, there were dozens of highly negative reviews about its quality and its potential. Obviously, Huffington overcame those initial bouts of failure and has cemented her name as one of the most successful outlets on the web.

2. **Bill Gates watched his first company crumble.** Bill Gates is now one of the world's wealthiest individuals, but he didn't earn his fortune in a straight line to success. Gates entered the

entrepreneurial scene with a company called Traf-O-Data, which aimed to process and analyze the data from traffic tapes (think of it like an early version of big data).He tried to sell the idea alongside his business partner, Paul Allen, but the product barely even worked. It was a complete disaster. However, the failure did not hold Gates back from exploring new opportunities, and a few years later, he created his first Microsoft product, and forged a new path to success.

3. George Steinbrenner bankrupted a team.
   Before Steinbrenner made a name for himself when he acquired ownership of the New York Yankees, he owned a small basketball team called the Cleveland Pipers back in 1960. By 1962, as a result of Steinbrenner's direction, the entire franchise went bankrupt.
   That stretch of failure seemed to follow Steinbrenner when he took over the Yankees in the 1970s, as the team struggled with a number of setbacks and losses throughout the 1980s and 1990s. However, despite public fear and criticism of Steinbrenner's controversial decisions, eventually he led the team to an amazing comeback, with six World Series entries between 1996 and

2003, and a record as one of the most profitable teams in Major League Baseball

4. Milton Hershey started three candy companies before Hershey's.
   Everyone knows Hershey's chocolate, but when Milton Hershey first started his candy production career, he was a nobody. After being fired from an apprenticeship with a printer, Hershey started three separate candy-related ventures, and was forced to watch all of them fail.
   In one last attempt, Hershey founded the Lancaster Caramel Company, and started seeing enormous results. Believing in his vision for milk chocolate for the masses, he eventually founded the Hershey Company and became one of the most well-known names in the industry.

5. Kenneth Chennault-CEO American Express
   The third African-American CEO of a Fortune 500 company, Kenneth Chenault has been the CEO of American Express since 2001. Another lawyer turned CEO, Chenault worked his way through the ranks at American Express — beginning in 1981. Also, an active public servant and recipient of the prestigious Third Lantern Award, Kenneth

Chenault has been likened to perennially successful business magnate, Jack Welch.

6. **Aliko Dangote-CEO-Dangote Group**
   The CEO of the eponymous Dangote group, this Nigerian businessman is the richest person of African descent in the world. Contributing to the development of Nigeria with the largest industrial conglomerate in West Africa, the Dangote Group employs upwards of 11,000 people, dealing with industries such as sugar refining, flour mills, food distribution, and cement. Also, a heavy contributor to political parties in the region, Dangote's businesses account for one-fourth of the Nigerian Stock Exchange.

7. **Robert L Johnson-CEO**
   Not only is he named after one of the most prolific blues musicians of all time, Robert L. Johnson is a true influencer of American culture and the first African-American billionaire. The former CEO of Black Entertainment Television provided for the world a voice and a vehicle for all things African-American: television shows, hip-hop, R&B, soul, and movies. Additionally, Johnson was the first African-American to head a company listed on

the New York Stock Exchange. Part owner of the Charlotte Bobcats, along with rapper Nelly and basketball giant Michael Jordan.

8. **Paul John Dejoria**
   As a first generation American, DeJoria had it rough from the beginning. His German and Italian parents divorced when he was two, and he sold Christmas cards and newspapers to help support his family before he turned 10. He was eventually sent to live in a foster home in Los Angeles. DeJoria spent some time as an L.A. gang member before joining the military. After trying his hand as an employee for Redken Laboratories, he took a $700 dollar loan and created John Paul Mitchell Systems. He hawked the company's shampoo door-to-door, living out of his car while doing so. But the quality of the product could not be denied, and now JPM Systems is worth over $900 million annually. He also created Patron Tequila and has a hand in a variety of industries, from diamonds to music.

9. Ursula Brown-Former CEO Xerox

Before the Lower East Side was cool, it was a hub for gangs. Burns was raised by her single mother in a housing project there. Her mother ran a day-care center out of her home and ironed shirts so that she could afford to send Ursula to Catholic school. She went to NYU, and from there became an intern at Xerox. She was the first African-American CEO woman to become the head of a Fortune 500 Company.

10. Leonardo Del Vecchio

Del Vecchio was one of five children who could not be supported by his widowed mother. After growing up in an orphanage, he went to work in a factory making molds for auto parts and eyeglass frames, where he lost part of his finger.

At 23, he opened his own molding shop. That eye-glass frame shop expanded to the world's largest maker of sunglasses and prescription eye ware. Luxottica makes brands like Ray-Ban and Oakley, with 6,000 retail shops like Sunglass Hut and Lens Crafters. His estimated net worth is now above $10 billion dollars.

11. J. K. Rowling

In the early 1990s, Rowling had just gotten divorced and was living on welfare with a dependent child. She completed most of the first "Harry Potter" book in cafes, as walking around with her daughter, Jessica, was the best way to get her to sleep.

The "Harry Potter" franchise has become a worldwide success and J.K. Rowling is now worth an estimated $1 billion.

Bibliography Page

1. **Scriptures were taken out of the King James Version (KJV & NLT & ESV) of the Holy Bible. Any scripture that did not come out of the King James Version, English Standard Version or New Living Translation, that version is stated by the scripture.**
2. **www.brainyquotes.com**
3. **Henry Louis Gates, Jr. Time Magazine, "Madam C.J. Walker: Her Crusade" December 7, 1998**
4. **Shawn Lim www.stunningmotivation.com**
5. **Willey Jolley, "A Set Back Is A Set-Up for A Comeback", October 12, 1999**
6. **Butterfly Life Cycle, www.thebutterflysite.com/lifecycle**
7. **Motivational Quotes, www.motivationping.com**
8. **Encouragement Quotes, http://www.quoteambition.com/best-encouraging-quotes-words-encouragement/**
9. **Jayson DeMers, Guest Writer, Success Stories (Arianna Huffington, Bill Gates, George Steinbrenner, Milton Hershey) December**

8, 2014 https://www.entrepreneur.com/article/240492

10. Business Insurance Quotes, 10 Most Successful African American CEOs of All Times, Staff Writer (Robert L Johnson, Aliko Dangote, Kenneth Chennault) http://www.businessinsurance.org/10-most-successful-african-american-ceos-of-all-time/
11. Success Quotes, 50 Best Success Quotes, http://under30ceo.com/50-best-success-quotes-of-all-time/
12. Business Insider, (John Paul Dejoria, Ursula Brown, Leonardo Del Vecchio, J.K. Rowling) 15 Inspirational -Rags To Riches Success Stories https://www.businessinsider.com/rags-to-riches-stories-2011-11

Contact Information:

1. **Virtue Consulting Company (Consulting Services and Business Services)**
   www.virtueconsultingco.com
   dth@virtueconsultingco.com
   240-676-3214

2. **Survivors Global Ministry (Non-Profit Organization) (Charitable Programs)**
   survivorsgm@gmail.com
   www.surivorsglobalministry.org
   240-676-3214

3. **Dr. DTH Ministries, Inc (Radio & TV; Books and Products, Other Services)**
   drdthministries@gmail.com
   deloresh30.wixsite.com/drdthministries
   240-676-3214

Mailing and Payment Location
P.O. Box 1544
Temple Hills, MD 20757

Office Location
6710 Oxon Hill Road, Suite 210
Oxon Hill, MD 20745